52

This is a collection of works of fiction. Names, characters, businesses, places, events and incidents are either the products of the author's imagination or used in a fictitious manner. Any resemblance to actual persons, living or dead, or actual events is purely coincidental. So if you think the poem is about you, I'm glad you connect with it, that's what a poem should do. You are not the only one on earth going through what you are going through, so share your own story and you never know who else you might help.

ISBN-10:0992361036
ISBN-13:978-0-9923610-3-7

She Fell Asleep on Australian Time
inspired by a 6 word story
by Jacqueline Thomas Rome

Prologue

A few years ago I was invited to a monthly poetry
night. What I didn't know then was that a few years
later I'd be looking forward to it each month, and
missing it the months that it wasn't on. Such wonderful
nights in the Australian bush with the open fire in the
mud brick home, everyone there invited by someone.

I was at a book launch recently and started reminiscing

a room of warm bodies
held together by words from the ages
not all poets, but all participants
lulled by the melody
enticed by the fire
seduced by the wine
verse leads to memory
memory to emotion
and emotion back to memories

Those nights will forever hold a special place not only
in my journey as a poet but in my life. It is for that
reason that I asked the host of all those wonderful
nights if she would do me the honor of writing the
forward for this latest collection.

Also Available

The Bard from Ballarat: Volume 1
The Bard from Ballarat: Volume 2
The Bard from Ballarat: International Edition
The Bard from Ballarat: Ebook Edition

Spoken Word CD's :

The Bard from Ballarat Southern Soliloquies
The Bard from Ballarat Southern Serenades

Anthologies Published in :

Moments in Time 2014
Poetry Pathways 2015
The Year of the Poet November 2014
The Year of the Poet December 2015
Aussie Words of Wisdom 2015
Aussie Words of Wisdom 2016

Songwriter on Album:

Love And Peace Is A Hammock
by Marie Ellen and the Londonderry duos

http://nevillehiatt.com

Gone

I see her in every drip
a letter of her name in every drop
I raise it to my nose
trying to breathe her back inside me
but she's gone
here no more

Forward
by Rona Lawrence

Having read this fine poetry, I am captured by it's call to lead me upwards ever upwards on a climb. A journey to what is good, to light, to dare I say it to God.

Only in love can man find his true purpose and I find it here in Neville's poetry, so strong, so compelling, inviting. I must follow and I will.

Contents

Freedom 2015

Can you hear me I'm trying to get through
Are you listening
Can you hear me filled with so many distractions
I'm trying to find a way in
I find a crack in your wall
but you fill it with mud
I find a gap in your armour
but you cover it up adding to your burden
I want to lighten your load
Why won't you let me through
I want to show you love
Why are your eyes looking elsewhere
I've been trying to get your attention
don't run,
don't hide
there is no need to be afraid
I want to give you freedom
Freedom from it all

Blue blood

Her wrists were dripping slits
as his words flowed through her bones
Reverberating in her mind
was everything he said
She wore her scars like a coat to stop their eyes
her body was now her own
but he still owned her mind

How do you live

How do you live with so little hope
How do you live with so much doubt
Just feel it
just
feel it
Your insecurities
The negative self talk
just feel it
be
open
peace and love, it is real
let the tears flow, release every blow
You are special
You are unique
be open and know the truth
let it go and be free
let
go
be
free
just be open and you will see
peace and joy will be found
a constant reminder that you are loved
beyond words
beyond thoughts
beyond actions
loved now and forever
loved like never before
loved like
never before

Make believe

No longer a girl wearing her mothers shoes
No longer a boy wearing his fathers tie
Now those heels are numbing her toes
and that tie feels like a noose around his neck

The teddies and dolls aren't packed away in boxes
As the day ends, they are held tighter than life itself
With kids of their own they don't see enough

What happened to those carefree days of make believe
When anything was possible if you just believed
Now the boss says what can and can't be done

No longer putting on her mothers makeup for fun
Now it's a struggle to find the time to put it on
No longer is his briefcase full of snacks
Now it's full of paperwork that will consume the entire
weekend

What happened to those carefree days of make believe
When anything was possible if you just believed

My Forever Friend

I thought you would never say goodbye
and now I feel too heavy to fly

I thought you would never say goodbye
and now I feel too heavy to fly

I thought love would be enough
I thought our friendship you would never snuff

Now I walk this path alone
Your number lies dormant in my phone

No more texts in the middle of the night
No more smiles brightening my sight

No more gifts on special days
Now I can only pray you will come to know his love

My arms no longer wrapped around you in a loving
embrace
Now folded in prayer, that you will lower your
defenses and let his healing hand dissolve those scars

Till The Voices Fall Silent

These voices are tearing me apart
Telling me I'm not good enough
and I'm not worth it

I hear you tell me I'm loved and precious
but the voices keep draggin me back
I feel your warm embrace
but these voices keep building walls blocking you out

Please hold me one more time
Tell me again how loved I am
Remind me one more time
Remind me that I am loved
Remind me that you love me

Hold me within your love
Till the walls fall down
and the voices fall silent

Please hold me one more time
Remind me again that you love me
Till the walls fall down
and the voices fall silent

Words

To some they are just letters on a page
To me they bubble up inside till they spill out in a
frenzied rage
Words just letters joined together, separated by spaces
Words connecting us together bringing us ever closer

Expressing how I feel, letting you see deep inside
but when I get no response I just want to run and hide
Why won't you let me in, is this just a game
I want to know you intimately
more than a title or name
My words appear to you on a screen
but they start in my heart
Will these words bring us together or draw us apart

Words just letters on a page
in you do they invoke love or rage
Words can describe so much, but are they enough to
stop you from escaping my clutch
Words in hundreds of languages and dialects

This page is but a mirror to my heart
Can you see what it reflects
Can you see yourself in its reflection
How much I love your unique complexion
Do you see how I feel
Can you see past what these words reveal

No Matter What

Man sees you naked
I see you clothed in my love

Man sees you as sex
I see you as my priceless creation

Man sees your most intimate parts
I see you most intimately

Man sees past your outer scars
I love you past your inner ones

Man lusts for your body
I love your soul

Man remembers you for but a moment
I have loved you since conception

Man wants you for a lifetime
I want you for eternity

Man wants to feast on your touch
I want to sustain you by my hand

Man longs to travel to be with you
I am with you always

Man wants you to walk through his door
My door will always be open to you

Man wants you to sleep with him
with Me you will always find rest

Man proclaims his love for you with words
I gave my life for you

I created man in my image
Just imagine how much more I can give you.

Falling

These chains wrapped around my heart
I feel them whether we're together or apart
Why can't I love you with all of me

What's holding me back

Constricted Constrained
What is causing this pain

I want to give you more
How do I pick up the slack
How do I take my life back

Where is the first link in this chain

This chain wrapped around my heart
Will it pull us apart

I want to be more
I know you deserve more
Constricted Constrained
What is causing this pain

On my knees I cry out
The chains loosen as I begin to shout
Constricted Constrained
Please set me free from this shame

On my knees I shout out aloud
is that the first link in the chain I just found

unraveling
falling away
as I continue to pray
crashing to the floor
dissolving in a pool of tears

melting away
disappearing along with my fears
these chains wrapped around my heart
I take a deep breath as they begin to depart

I'm on my feet running free
Soaring through the trees
I'm on my feet standing tall
Knowing on my knees is a safe place to fall

I found a safe place to fall
and now I'm standing taller than I ever have before

The Greatest Man

From the greatest man you've ever known
and thoughts of how much you've grown
To staring at your pictures
filling my suitcase of memories

From I love you forever
to I won't see you again ever

This suitcase is getting heavier

From blond to brown, thick to thin
the gaps in this suitcase are filling in

Short to tall I've kissed them all
Over the years one after another they all seem to fall

pictures
poems
cards

all but markers in time

Two garter belts

Who's they were God only knows
So many thoughts fill my head
Yet I lay alone in my queen sized bed
Mementos marking chapters of my life

I'd happily give up this suitcase

Just for one introduction to my wife

Love Song

I heard all the songs on the radio
Love
Loss
and everything in between
but they were just words till I met you

Words on the radio
On the screen and in my head
Love and loss and the price of the cost
but they were just words on a page
Till I met you

Now I know what they mean
those songs of love
more beautiful than the morning sun
They are about you

The words of loss and longing
sung about the distance between us

Now when I hear the songs on the radio
I think of you

When I'll next see you
When I'll next get to hear your voice
to smell your hair

Oh my dear, my love
You came into my life
and now
I'm singing those songs on the radio

You are the ink in my pen
and the plectrum for my guitar

Now people are singing songs about you
and they are all on the radio

Questions

How much time do you spend looking in the mirror to
impress your boss
Have you taken the time to look in your colleagues
cubicle to see them on the verge of suicide due to their
recent loss

How much attention do those games on your phone get
Do you touch your partner enough to even make them
sweat

How many times a week do you buy a latte
How often does a child go unsponsored because you
say not today

How many of your neighbours even know your first
name
Or are you too busy updating your status to garnish
hollow fame

When was the last time you sent someone a card in the
mail
Or are you to busy watching videos of yet another epic
fail

Did you even listen to the question when you
answered no
Who will be around to help you when your hair turns
to snow

S

She'll never know how much it meant to me
So in the moment there was no need to flee

Just one night
One hour
Yet for that moment in time
Something grew in me like the most beautiful flower

Today I wake in tears
but it's because she calmed my fears

Such a priceless gift she offered up
Such a rewarding way to fill my cup

As her heartbeat slowed to but a flutter
Mine
Well my heart
It melted like butter

Your Voice

Please say my name

I long to hear it from your lips one more time
please drown me in your voice

I want to feel you as I close my eyes

No distractions just you and me

lost in the ocean of your lips

to make it last

just a little sip

please just say my name one more time

one syllable

a consonant

a vowel

My fingers tingle as your lips move

Your tongue forms the first sound and I quiver

I'm shaking,

I'm a mess

and then there it is

My name

Your voice

Oops

When I heard the news you had whiplash
My heart just crashed

Being this far away from you
Too far away to help you through

Uncle Sam sent me away to many yesterdays
Just know that every time I think of you I feel sun rays

My heart warms with every letter you send
I just wish I was there to help you mend

Thank God you got out alive
I thank God you got out alive

When I heard the news you had whiplash
my heart just crashed

Cuts and bruises because he ran a red light
I'm just so glad you're going to be alright

I never knew quite how to say how much you meant to
me
but staring death in the face has set me free

I no longer care what anyone else thinks
I certainly don't care if a professor thinks my writing
stinks

I need you to know how empty my life would be if
you went away
and I need to say it, while it's still today

I need to convey how I feel
How much to me you matter
Despite the miles I pray you can hear what I say

Tomorrow may be my last
Though I hope it's not

Tonight I'm dreaming of laying down my past
and giving you all I've got
Laying here in my bed
With your picture not two feet from my head

When I heard the news you had whiplash
My heart just crashed

Thank God you got out alive

I thank God you got out alive

Does She Love Me, or Does She Love Me Not

If I planted a rose for every tear I've cried since you've
been gone I'd have a garden as beautiful as you

If I had a dollar for every day you weren't here I'd buy
you a diamond ring and ask you to stay

If I wrote a poem for every time I thought of you I
could build a staircase to the moon

Where did you go

What did you see

I don't care who he was
or what he did
or didn't do

All that matters is that you know
I still want you
My love for you has not waned
Though I know it all to be in vain

I know you will leave again
and in between you'll drive me round the bend

But I don't care
This thing you do
No one else has done

It is for you
and you alone
That I write about the setting sun

You turn my grass blue
and the sky green

I know not how but you strengthen me to lift a car
nay a bus
a train
You fuel my fire so hot I could melt a plane

I long to see new pictures
to see how much you've changed

Your old ones though by my bed
are still branded in my brain

I could write till my fingers were numb
and it wouldn't be enough

Your back for now and so this first rose I pluck

does she love me

or does she love me not?

BBQ

I thought the BBQ smelt good

till you sat down next to me

flowers in the wind

my eyes closing in glee

a tropical island

the waves crashing on the shore

I tilted my head

I wanted more

a summer breeze

sugar in my brain

seeping into my veins

you shift

I move

my lungs need to stay full

you turn

I feel the pull

Blue French Horn Forever

I spent years listening to your song
but now the last note has been played

You weaved a tune so captivating
I held my breathe between each verse

Wondering what tale the next section would tell

I laughed
I cried
I even high fived

All in all it's been
legendary

So many hooks over the years
Kept me coming back for more
but now the final note has been played

Promises were made and friendships challenged
Yet the whole world tuned in
as you took your final bow

Love wove it's unpredictable hand throughout
The city skyscape changed in the time
it took to tell your tale

and now that the curtains have closed
Your memory will live on in the hearts
and minds that witnessed it all

Blue french horn forever

The Quilt of Memories

She sat on the beach a quilt on her lap

Every square evoking a memory from her life

The honeymoon

Her husband

Her son

all but memories now

no grandchildren

nothing but this quilt left

Her eyes once sparkled like the ocean

Now her hair the color of the white sand

A quilt full of memories

Love, the thread holding them all together

The flowers on her husbands grave

The medal awarded to her son after the war

Every square a marker in time

Each memory as precious as the next

Childhood

She was born to children
Yet she never had a childhood

Escaping into other worlds inside a book

Hiding away where no one else would look

Her classmates called her by name
it was defeat

She painted pictures in her head

Holding her teddy tight
To keep away the fright from the night

From a little girl to a woman
teddy never left her bed

As she continued to paint pictures in her head

Then one day she took a stand
and picked up a paintbrush in her hand

Now no longer called defeat
critics are throwing accolades at her feet

No longer curled up in tears on the floor
She watches as the auction prices continue to soar

She wields the brush like a sword
and now her inner child lives in harmonious accord

She still paints pictures in her head

Except now they hang over someone else's bed

From Your Soul To My Heart

I'd play this guitar till my fingers wept
If it would change how you felt

I'd harvest the amazon to print enough sheet music
If it would change how you feel

I'd sing until I could no longer whisper

I'd sing until you felt something shift deep inside

The moon would turn from full to new
and I'd keep writing songs for you

If it would change your world
I'd learn to dance and play the violin

I'd do it all
If it would help the sun shine through

I'd play this guitar till my fingers wept
If it would change how you felt

I'd replant the amazon to print enough sheet music
If it would help you heal

I'd do all this and more
To help you up off that floor

I'd play till my fingers wept

if it would change how you feel

Sober

There was a drink in her hand
after every night with the band

Soon that drink felt better in her hand than her guitar
yet everyone was still telling her she was a star

Not yet old enough to vote or fight
Yet the war was raging on
and she was losing the battle

A drink with the band
progressed to not being able to stand

She was a run away chart success
but without a liquid breakfast she never felt her best

They were still calling her a star
even when she totaled her brand new car

Laying in the hospital bed
a metal plate replacing the bone in her head

The shakes were the worst part
but it was only the start
The rehab took years,
but a lot of growth was achieved through all those
tears

Now she is back singing songs from her heart

3 years sober and old enough to fight
It's still a daily battle but she is winning the war

Her guitar sings her stories
and she is changing lives with every chord

She doesn't care what the tabloids say
Laying in that hospital bed she remembered how to
pray

Now when her songs hit the charts
She is just thankful she was given a second start.

My Angel Underground

The wheels on this bus keep going round and round

but where is my heart to be found

I've traveled east and west

Yet I can't find a place where my heart can find rest

Please draw me a map so I can find that spot

Melt my heart so it feels warmth again

You're an angel underground

No more giggles in my ear

or bedtime stories to scare away that night time fear

Your photos sit silent,

Your paintings are fading fast

These tears are carving channels in my face

My soul still yearns to share just one more sunrise
with you

Sitting on the beach feeling the sand between our toes

but you're my angel underground no longer to be
found

All those years ahead we could have had together

All those years ahead we would have had together

but now you're my angel underground

and I no longer hear a sound

Just Once

I've dreamt of hearing you say it

Since the first moment we met

Wondering what it would take

to release that sound from your mouth

Where would we be when your throat

finally made that offering to my ears

Would I be close enough

to feel your breath on me

as your lips parted

Would my heart skip a beat

as the inflection in your voice

melts the synapses of my brain

Will I hear it a second time straight away

or will you leave me wondering

Just once

I want to feel you say it

just once

Rainbows

If emotions were colours in a rainbow

Then I've felt them all

joy, sadness, pity, and pain

How dull life would be if the sun didn't reflect off the rain

That smell of new life

washing away a world of strife

The colours of a rainbow

my life will never be the same

The hue of blue

there with me my whole life through

The strength of green promising new futures

The brightness of yellow

shining through the darkest of storms

The warmth of orange

letting me rest in it's peace

The fullness of red

reminding me to live life in love

And purple

constantly reassuring me I was born for more than this

As I bathe in the pot of Gold

at the end of all these emotions

I'm reminded it doesn't matter who you are

or what you've done

or what's been done to you

It only matters what you do with your rainbow

today

I am Rose

My life is as a Rose

Starting of a young sapling

Weak and impressionable

and as I grow thorns develop

to protect me from the ills of the world

but every season I bloom and blossom

and bring a colour and fragrance to my world

like only I was born to do

Every winter I have to hibernate

and rebuild my strength for the next season

Sometimes I need pruning

that I may grow that much stronger in the years ahead

Though disease may try to attack me

I vow to fight on

Year after year growing ever stronger

So each year as the first rays of the springtime sun

warm the winter frost from my leaves

I may once more burst forth

With colour and fragrance

Brightening the world in which I live

Flowers 2014

I want to see you in nothing but your smile

I want to see every flaw

every feature

every memory

every thought

every feeling

I want to see what you've kept hidden all these years

don't be shy

don't be coy

I've seen more than most will ever know

but in this splice in history

I want to see you

show me who you truly are

I want to see every scar

when I wake in the morning and gaze in the mirror

I want to see the real you

If Wishes Were My Friend

If wishes were my friend
I'd introduce him to you

If wishes were my friend
I'd beseech them to be kind to you

I'd wish for the sun to always warm your heart
I'd wish for your friends to never depart

I'd wish for a roof over your head
I'd wish for fresh clean sheets for your bed

But most of all I'd wish you knew real true love
The kind I know dumped down from above

For if you knew this love to be true
you'd never need another wish your whole life through

Though I be broken and poor
I know he is always there to pick me up
right off the floor

if wishes were my friend

if wishes were my friend.

Lucy

She came into my life without a care
Till cancer took away every wisp of her hair

A pink beanie on her head
Her mothers chair next to her bed

Lucy came into my life, her room full of fresh flowers
laying in that bed with her little stuffed bear

No amount of drugs could eradicate that smile
That smile that brightened the world even outside of
those walls

Sadly cancer won the race
but that smile
That smile never left her face

Lucy came into my life for a reason of that I am sure
before she fell asleep she slipped a note into my hand

It read

"it's ok to cry
this is but a temporary goodbye"

my knees hit the floor

for I could stand no more

I read the last line

"I will see you again
thank you for being my friend"

Journeys

Take a good long look at this guitar
every nick, every dent, every scratch
they all tell a story

Journeys of my life
of friends no longer here
of loves left behind

Take a good long look at this guitar
but please be kind
this is my heart, my life, my soul

Putting new strings on this guitar
doesn't make me whole
I could sand it back and make it look like new
but I'm afraid you'd still see through

Every nick, every dent, every scratch
have a look inside each one
and see a chapter of my life

Of dreams shattered, and hopes unfulfilled
but through it all there was you

Putting bandages on my fingers
when I played till they bled
Pulling the covers up when I fell asleep
writing a new song in your bed

There for me long after the last fan had left
The records and the trophies never changed a thing
You were always there ready to hand me a new string

I am

If the saying what doesn't break you only makes you stronger were true then

I am Hera for I have survived divorce

I am Mars for I have survived being raped

I am Isis for I have survived miscarriage

I am Anubis for I have lost loved ones

I am Demeter for I have survived a drought

I am Fortuna for I have survived financial ruin

I am Mercury for I have survived being kidnapped

I am Apollo for I was born deaf

I am Poseidon for I have survived a flood

I am Vulcan for I have survived bush fires

I am Ares for I have survived war

but if truth be told

I am merely human

and this is life

She fell asleep on Australian time

She fell asleep on Australian time
A baby in her arms
A ring on her finger
neither were there last week

She fell asleep on Australian time
Her only child 10,000 miles away
Her knees more worn than ever before
their lives forever altered

She fell asleep on Australian time
Dreaming of a land she has never been
Praying for his safe return
stroking his head, telling him he is loved

She fell asleep on Australian time
The letter well worn from being read
The first rays now lighting her bed
Entrusting him to someone else's care
the cover of her bible now worn bare

The Heart Knows

I don't need eyes to know your beautiful

I don't need feet to walk in your shoes

I don't need fingers to hold your hand

All I need is this heart

to feel yours

The fame

You think you know my name
but all you know is the fame
the magazines
the newspapers
the press
you think you know my name
but all you know is the fame
the tabloids
the pictures
the hype
just one side of the coin
behind closed doors another story unfolds

Saving Grace

I don't want the fame or the fortune

I just want them to know

Let them forget my name
Let them forget my words

I just want them to know

Let my books go out of print
Let my Cd's never be played

I just want them to know

I found hope
I found peace

I just want them to know

I found hope
I found peace

I just want them to know

Let the press ignore me
Let my agent fire me

I just want them to find you

I just want them to know you

Mirror Mirror

mirror mirror please change me
I don't like what I see

mirror mirror please
make me beautiful
take away my curves
make these scars disappear

mirror mirror please
change me
I don't like what I feel
wipe away these tears
I feel so small
please give me a new name

mirror mirror stop showing me this reflection
take me to a land where their words don't reach
take me to a land where people live by what they teach
I just want to be anywhere but here

If I give you my beauty
will you share it with the world?
If I dry your tears
will you comfort others living in fear?
If I took you away
who would reflect me for all to see?

mirror mirror I don't understand
I feel like I'm in sinking sand
How can I reflect your beauty
look at me

I see beauty
and a loving heart beyond measure
I see compassion
and inspiration for those barely able to cope
I see hope beyond those fears
I see joy beyond your tears

Mirror Mirror I'll give it one more day
Thank you for showing me your reflection
Thank you for giving me courage to stay

I Am With You Always

It doesn't matter what they do or say
I am with you always

Sticks and stones didn't break my bones
It was a hand that nailed me to that tree

I feel the pain in your eyes
I hear those silent tears
I am with you always

I could stop the bullies hand
I could cork the drunkards bottle
but where would the intervention stop

Man wants to feast on your touch
I want to sustain you by my hand
Man longs to travel to be with you
I am with you always

Man wants you to walk through his door
My door will always be open to you
Man wants you to sleep with him for a night
I am with you always

I could silence the angry parent
and destroy all the drugs
but where would the intervention stop

It doesn't matter what they do or say
Just remember where I learnt to pray

Fairy Tales (duet)

I could dance with Cinderella
Kiss Sleeping Beauty or
Brush Rapunzel's hair
but I'd rather be right here with you

I could kiss a frog
Ride away on a white horse
or fly to never never land
but I'd rather be right here with you

You are the sun and the stars

You are the ocean and the moon

I could bake you a house
Storm a castle
or fly into space
but I'd still rather be right here with you

I could fly on a magic carpet
Make a little boys wish come true
or swim in the ocean
but I'd still rather be right here with you

You are the love that stood the test of time

You are the love that stood the test of time

I could slay a dragon
Rob the rich
or give a lion his courage

I could eat a mushroom
Click my shoes together
or sleep in a bed that's just right

I could do it all but without you I might as well let my
house be blown over
For you are the belle of my ball

I could do it all but without you all the golden straw in
the world would be worthless
For you are the one I want to read of every night

You are the sun and the stars
You are the love that stood the test of time

You are the ocean and the moon
You are the love that stood the test of time

A Woman in Love

I never noticed you

until someone else already had

I never felt your beauty

until someone else showed you how much

Your smile never caught my eye

until you were all they could see

A woman in love how bright you shine

Now I know of your compassion and grace

before I never even knew your name

Now you are taking someone else's

6

6 chambers
1 bullet
drugs
danger
chance
fear
you

Flowers

Where are the flowers

my name

well let's be real

even if I told you

you wouldn't remember it tomorrow

as I hide in these bushes

that grab and tear at my flesh I ask

Where are the flowers

as I see my mother being raped

and my father slaughtered like a ram

I ask where are their flowers

as bullets cut through my village like a meteor attack

I ask where are their flowers

you live in such safety

and I'd say spend a day in my shoes

except I have none

I gave them to my best friend before they took him

you see he could run faster that way

but they still caught him

you spend more on that one bunch of flowers

than my family sees in a year

so I ask you

are those flowers really for them

or are they for you?

If We Really Loved Without Borders

If we really loved without borders how would we live

Would you see my heart before the clothes I wear

Would I need to lock my car to keep you out

or would my home always be open to you

Would there be children going hungry

while I buy a bigger tv

Would we be flying to the moon

when a mother has to walk for days for fresh water

If we really loved without borders

The Promised Land

The promised land

Where dreams are reality

The movies, TV and magazines all selling

all giving you things to fill a hole

the sex

the drugs

the money

the rock and roll

and I'm not talking about the ads

the latest diet

or hippest do dads

I'm talking about what you set you PVR for

I'm talking about what you ignore the phone for

and behind this thin veneer are the homeless

the ones that gave their all

behind the fast cars, bright lights and parties

the ones in a hotel room alone and cold

behind the success stories, the heroes and celebrities

are those making their final choice

to leave the promised land

behind the overnight success and the next big thing

Is someone holding life or death in their hands.

Memories 2014

From the lady at the lake

To not being able to cry at my boyfriends wake

They were all just moments in time to get me to you

From a marriage

To a miscarriage

just stepping stones in my life

and now here I am ready to spend a moment with you

A moment that may end before this poem does

A moment that may have a multitude of many
moments

Each one as momentous as the last

The moments before you I would not change

I am who I am because of these moments

I want to create memories with you because of your
moments

You will look different after this moment ends

But it is your inner shaping and moulding that makes
me want to spend each and every moment with you

These moments in time

Are worth my very last dime

Knock knock

Shaking on the floor

loves knocking on the door

curled up the size of a flea

my tears a whispered plea

shivering and shaking

loves thumping so hard

the walls are moving in

waiting

pulling the curtains shut

as love tries to shine in

sleeping through the day

eating too much

love slips a note under the door

the dishes pile up

the carpet gets dirty

yet love waits patiently

waiting for the curtains to be closed no more

waiting for the door to open

waiting for you to feel the grass underfoot

waiting to caress the tears from your face

waiting to warm you from the inside out

eternally

waiting

Notes on a Page

Just lines on the page

Ink on paper

Connecting the dots

Giving them a place to call home

Caressing them

Supporting them

Giving them voice

Aiding performance

or perceived comprehension

Value

Duration

Supplication or

Suffocation

Notes on a page

medicating my soul

Stone

He needed her to stop his heart from turning to stone

Yet the only way she could do that was to tear it in two

Jagged edges rough and raw

Bleeding

Trying to heal

Trying to join back together

Soft and pliable

Compassionate and humble

He needed her to exist

So he could live outside of his head

Holding her till her dam wall broke

Holding her till it was breathe or choke

Mingled and intertwined

yet worlds apart

the distance of a heart

Stary Night

The stars above your head

metal bars form your comforting bed

a million dollar view

so far removed from the world you once knew

Exiled

Salt the taste of your absence in my life

The longer you're gone the harder it gets

I'm so sad it's like I have the flu
But no I'm just that blue
I'm missing you

Everywhere I look you're there
Haunting my world with your hair

We were so close

You pulled away and then

We got even closer

and now nothing

Cut off

Exiled

I want to call you so bad
To visit and see your face

But you've said
You no longer want me occupying that space

You let me in so far
I saw what others haven't

Yet I didn't run
I didn't hide

I sat with you through it all
Yet you no longer want me to call

I don't know what to do

So I beg and plead, because I know you have a need

I pray that despite what I saw
You will one day reopen that door

Your walls are keeping out love as well

So I drop to my knees

and cry for your loss, and your pain

I cry for what you didn't get

I cry for what you don't have

My heart aches as the tears flow

The pain you must have felt

to tell me to go

Yet here I remain

still feeling for you

In His Arms

Your arms are open

and though I can enter their embrace

I cannot fill them

I cannot meet the need you are trying to sate

I am but another face

Another name

His arms are open

Longing to have you in them

His loving embrace can bare the weight of your past

Where others arms stole your preciousness

He wants to meet your needs

He wants you to feel loved

Salvation

The keys are stiff

The hues of ebony and ivory
are almost indistinguishable

Spiders run across the octaves
without making a sound

The strings are rusted
their tautness has waned

The detail of the wood grain
obscured by years of dust

A butterfly lands on a fret
in silence

A gentle touch, a loving hand
soft fingers, a caring heart

Restoration giving way
to revitalization

A sweet melody blowing

away the final cobwebs

Through His Eyes

Through his eyes
I see compassion and hope
I see a reason to live
I see so many opportunities to give

Through his eyes
I see the world differently
I see needs I can meet
I see hearts yearning for more

Through his eyes
My life is wonderful
My life is ending
but today is ......

Today is another chance
To feel loved and share it
To know that before I go to bed tonight
I could
Save someone's life

Today is another opportunity
To be a shoulder to cry on
To be a caring ear

Today these fingers can type
An encouragement that might
just give someone enough to say

tomorrow

Do you like stories longer than a poem ….

Some Shorter than Others

A collection of short stories for the young and young at heart

Neville Hiatt
Illustrated by Sylvia Hollis

Algunas mas cortas que otras

Una colección de historias cortas para el joven y el joven de corazón

Neville Hiatt
Ilustrado por Sylvia Hollis
Traducido por Luis Montoya

Algumas
mais curtas
que outras

Uma coleção de histórias para o jovem e o jovem de coração

Neville Hiatt

Ilustrações por Sylvia Hollis
Tradução por Patricia Fischer

Einige
kürzer
als
andere

Eine Geschichtensammlung für Junge und Junggebliebene.

Neville Hiatt

Illustriert von Sylvia Hollis
Übersetzt von Viktor Isaak

well some of them are ....

man I feel like a ..

I just feel
for so long ... nothing
and now .... I can't stop

www.ingramcontent.com/pod-product-compliance
Lightning Source LLC
Chambersburg PA
CBHW021240090426
42740CB00006B/627